Create an Alter Ego for Work Success and Peace of Mind

Charles Mage

Published by Charles Mage, 2022.

CREATE AN ALTER EGO FOR WORK SUCCESS AND PEACE OF MIND

First edition. August 14, 2022.

Copyright © 2022 Charles Mage.

ISBN: 979-8201785383

Written by Charles Mage.

Also by Charles Mage

Magickal Imagination: Learn to Use Your Imagination in a
Magickal and Witchy Way
Dowsing the Casino: Make Money Dowsing
Magickal Partnership
Energy Ball Manual
Sex Magick for the Solitary Practitioner
Elemental Invocation
Vampirism Magick for Beginners
Vril Mastery: Harness the Force of the Gods
Psi Constructs
The Magickal Mindset
Instant Magick for Everyday Use
Healing with Psi
Magick as a Way of Life
Dowsing Without Tools
Learn to Create an Astral Temple
Fun Things to Do with Your Energy Ball
In Search of Beauty
Imagination Magick: Learn to Use Your Imagination to Live a
Magickal Life
Pendulum Magick: Communicate with Spirits
Magick in Your Pocket: Magical Spells You Can Cast
Anywhere, Even in Your Pocket!

Make Your Own Magick Wand The Intuitive Way
The Way of the Magus
The Secret Occult Techniques of Making and Using a Ouija
Board
Mistakes and Pitfalls in Magical Practice
The Magick of the Zenina Circle
Escape Life with Your Imagination
Experiments with Magical Energy
Elemental Magick of the Five Fingers
Magical Keys to Self-Empowerment
How to Acquire & Take Care of Magickal Creatures
Beat the Casino Using Clairvoyance
The Magical Art of Mental Projection
Mindcraft Spells Starter Manual
The Magick of the Holy Rosary
How the Rosary Changed My Life and How It Can Change
Yours Too
True Initiation into the Craft of Magick
The Way of the Pendulum
The Christian Magician
Shamanic Journey for Beginners
Life Lessons from a Butterfly
Psychokinesis Manual to Beat the Casino and Make Money
Phone Sex Magick
The Magick of Writing
Energy Servitor Manual
My Magickal Rosary Journey
How to Create an Elemental Servitor
Basic Wizardry 101
Create an Alter Ego for Work Success and Peace of Mind

Watch for more at https://www.charlzdelacruz.com/.

Table of Contents

Overview 1

What is an Alter Ego? 3

Do You Need an Alter Ego? 5

Benefits of Having an Alter Ego 7

How to Play the Game 11

Creating and Programming Your Alter Ego 13

Activating Your Alter Ego 17

Playing the Role of Your Alter Ego 19

Shifting Back to Your True Self 23

Make Adjustments to Your Alter Ego 25

Time Management 27

Non-Attachment 29

Should You Tell People About Your Alter Ego? 33

"Real" Life Game 35

Can You Create More Than One Alter Ego? 37

How to Be Happy As Your Alter Ego 39

On Spirituality 41

A Message 43

About the Author 45

For Katie, Liz, & J.

Overview

Create an *Alter Ego for Work Success and Peace of Mind* is a life manual that teaches the secrets of creating a different persona or your alter ego to handle all the work for you. Are you being bombarded with so much stress and pressures at work? Are you having a hard time dealing with people at work? Have you realized that you cannot be your true self at work? Do you want to be more efficient and effective at work? Does your real personality conflict with the personality that you need for work? If you have answered yes to any of these questions, then this book is for you.

Creating an alter ego is a great way to manage stress and all the work that you do. This way, all the negative energies will be handled by your alter ego as your real self remains pure and undefiled by the modern world. Yes, this is something that you can do, and all it takes is a shift in your mindset and the way you view things.

These days, many professionals are sad and unsatisfied with their work. Work has become so stressful and problematic that it is no longer fun. By creating an alter ego, things will be a lot more manageable for you, and you will no longer be directly affected by the stresses and pressures of your work.

Create an Alter Ego for Work Success and Peace of Mind teaches the ins and outs of creating an alter ego that can help you with your work, but you can also apply the same technique to help you with other matters of your life. But, this book is focused on work-related matters. Indeed, by the time that you finish reading this book, you will have the power to create an alter ego that will allow you to live your best life.

I learned about this technique when my life got very stressful. I am a professional who engages directly with people, helping them resolve their problems. After some time, I realized that I was already suffering, and I was suffering really badly. I was earning more money but my level of happiness was almost gone. I became depressed and extremely vulnerable that even my family was already being affected. But, once I learned to create an effective alter ego, I became untouchable to the stresses of work, and I returned back to my true self—happy and peaceful all the time. This book has been written to help share what I have learned, so that if you are also caught in the same or similar challenges in life, then here is the way out—a key to power and a way to true happiness and peace of mind.

What is an Alter Ego?

An alter ego is your other self. Think of Superman and Clark Kent or Bruce Wayne and Batman. Another good example would be Peter Parker and Spiderman. By dividing the self into two (or more, if necessary—but only to two is what I strongly recommend), you can manage your life and all the things and work that you have to do more effectively without sacrificing your peace of mind and true self-identity.

Your alter ego is someone who would do all the work and take all the pain and hardships for you. This way, your true self will remain pure and uncorrupted by the work environment. It also functions like a shield that protects you during work and all the negative energies that come with it.

The good news is that creating an alter ego is easy to do as long as you know the proper way to do it. As you read this book, all that I ask is you keep an open mind. You do not need to believe in whatever that I tell you. Instead, you are encouraged to just consider these ideas and see for yourself if these would be helpful for you or not. But, just so you know, all the knowledge that you would learn from this book are all based on real-life facts and personal experiences.

An alter ego is someone that you can create. This is not entirely new. In fact, we have been creating alter egos every now and then, but most of the time we do it unconsciously. For example, how you are with your friends might be different from the way that you are with your family. How you behave when you are in front of your boss might be different from the way you are with your friends. There are, of course, many other examples that we can give to show how certain alter egos are created by people unintentionally.

When you create your alter ego intentionally, it will become much more effective and powerful. This way, you can consciously control the alter ego that you are creating, and you can make adjustments to its personality where necessary. This time, you can be in full control instead of just always reacting to how the external world affects you. This is an effective way to stop being a victim of the modern world. By creating an alter ego, you can protect and keep who you really are. You can keep yourself pure and undefiled, as nothing in the workplace can touch you. You will be invincible. You will be free. You can finally be you, free and happy.

Do You Need an Alter Ego?

Before you go about creating your alter ego, it is good to ask first if this is really something that you need. If you are one of the lucky ones, perhaps you do not need to create an alter ego at all; but for many of us, it would be very helpful to have an alter ego. It is a way of protection and self-preservation. I personally know many professionals who are regularly consulting with psychiatrists because the stress and pressures of work have become too unbearable for them. Their souls have been suffering for much too long that they are sad and unhappy with their life despite any success in their career. Some of them seem to act tough and happy, but deep inside, they know that there is something wrong as they are hurt, and they cease to be who they truly are.

If you are happy with your work and you think that you do not need any adjustments or protection, that you can just be who you really are and things would be well and good, then you are lucky, indeed. In this case, you may not need an alter ego—consider yourself very lucky. However, for a good number of us, especially when the work involves dealing with people (especially with difficult people), then having an alter ego would be extremely helpful.

It is also possible that your real personality may not match well with the kind of personality that your work demands. In this case, your work may suffer if you continue to be the very kind *you*. Sometimes you may need to *act* tough and strict even if that is not who you really are, just so you can be more effective in the work that you do. In this case, having an alter ego would be very beneficial for you.

Whether or not you need an alter ego would depend on your personal circumstances, as well as how you are currently managing all the work stress and work-related problems. If you want, just give having an alter ego a try, and see how it works for you.

Benefits of Having an Alter Ego

Let us now discuss the benefits of having an alter ego. Having an alter ego is something that could be very beneficial and helpful for you. It has many practical benefits. Let us examine them one by one:

Effective Protection

Having an alter ego is an effective form of protection. It can keep your real self pure and untouched by your work and all those people that you deal with. Instead of you having to face and deal with them, you can give that difficult task to your alter ego, and let your alter ego handle all those problems for you.

Having an alter ego is having a thick layer of protection. Imagine a world where the real you would be undefiled and untouched by the world around you. It is a beautiful and wonderful world. And, here is the kicker: This is something that you can do right now at this very moment.

The truth is that even if you try to just relax and not be affected by the people at your workplace and all the work that you are doing, you are only human—and you will be affected. This is also the reason why so many professionals these days are very much stressed out and unhappy. Some even reach a point where they could not handle it anymore and end their own lives by their own hand (but never let the world make you do this). If the world strikes you, be sure to stand strong and strike it harder. Be strong, be courageous—you deserve a good and happy life.

Become More Effective at Work

Having an alter ego can also help you become more effective at work. You can match your alter ego with the right personality and attitude that you need with what the nature of your work demands. When you create your alter ego intentionally and consciously, then you can also exercise the power to make conscious adjustments to what your alter ego would be like. Does your work need you to become stricter and more formal? Then you can easily make an alter ego to fit that standard. Does your work need you to be more patient and respectful even when facing difficult and disrespectful people? Then you can create a perfect alter ego for that specific purpose, and so on. Your alter ego can fit into any situation that you may need to deal with, thereby increasing efficiency and productivity.

Be More Flexible

When you create an alter ego, you get to exercise full control over what your alter ego would be like. You can control how it reacts to certain things, how it should behave and talk to people, and so on. Indeed, you have complete control over it, and you can even make adjustments over time whenever necessary to better fit the changing and endless demands of your profession. So, depending on what you may need for work, you can customize your alter ego to be what it needs to be for you to successfully meet the demands of your work with the highest efficiency and effectiveness.

Be Free from Stress

When you have an alter ego, you will no longer have to be stressed over the things that happen at work. Rather, it is your

CREATE AN ALTER EGO FOR WORK SUCCESS AND PEACE OF MIND

alter ego's job to handle all those matters. You can just keep yourself who you really are and let your alter ego be the one to face all those worries. In fact, since your alter ego is just your creation, your alter ego would not even need to worry for it is not a very personal creation in the sense that it may not feel a thing, depending on how you program your alter ego. So, the next time you feel any stress at work, just let that stress go by passing it on to your alter ego who may not have any sensitivity to stress, thereby allowing you to focus on the problems just as they are and come up with a more practical and best course of action to resolve the issues, whatever they may be.

I know many people who like to say that work stress should not affect them as a person. After all, it is all just work, right? However, they only manage to be successful at this in their dreams. In real life, they are very pissed and sad that they even end up taking stress medications and the likes. Never allow yourself to be like them. Instead, you can create an alter ego who will handle all the stress for you and would even solve your work-related problems and also do all the work for you.

You will be able to Think and Feel from Outside the Box

When you have an alter ego, the workplace becomes the environment of the game. Since you will be playing as your alter ego and not as your real self, you will be able to think and feel outside the box. Your work is just like a game inside a box. This will allow you to view the game from different angles and from a fresh perspective. This would be very helpful for practical reasons, as well as for your own peace of mind.

You will Learn Not to Take Time for Granted

Having an alter ego and going through this experience will help you realize the importance of every moment and why you should not take time for granted. Many people go through life without being grateful for each day that they receive. Each day is a gift, and every moment is a miracle. You will realize this usually when you know that the time for your true self has to take a break as you will have to switch to your alter ego to deal with worldly matters. From now on, be sure to make every moment count, especially the time that you spend as your true self.

Take Control of Your Life

When you create an alter ego, you can gain control of your life. The bad and negative parts can be handled by your alter ego while you keep your true self and identity just the way you want. Since you will be creating your alter ego, you can make it as good as you want it. It is your own artistic creation. As for your personal life with your true self, it will remain unblemished and well under your control. You will no longer be a victim to the world. As for your personal life, it will be as you want it to be. Let your alter ego handle all the work, as well as all the dramas and complications that come with it as you keep your true self pure and happy.

How to Play the Game

You have to understand that work is like a game. In fact, our life is like a big game. When you create an alter ego, it is good that you have this understanding. It is technically not a game but it works very much like a game to the point that there are people out there who view life literally as a game. Now, do not get me wrong, just because you view it as a game does not mean that it is petty or meaningless. If you love your life, then it is wonderful.

When you make an alter ego, you have to do it correctly to make it effective, as well as to make the most of it. You are probably familiar with role-playing games. Creating an alter ego is the same where you need to create and define your character for the game. Once you set your character, you can start giving life to it, and then that character (your alter ego) can now start doing its purpose and make life much easier and happier for you.

You will be having to concrete selves: your true identity (the real you) and your alter ego. Of course, your alter ego is also you, but take it as the self that is not related to your true self. Your alter ego is simply the character that you will be roleplaying as in the game. Treat your work as the game—things would be much easier this way—and your alter ego is your character.

When you have an alter ego, you will be having dual lives. Your true self will continue to live the way you really want to live your life while your alter ego will handle the other stuff—mostly the stuff that you do not like and all the work that you must do. You have to get used to this separation of identity. In the beginning, this may be a challenge, but just give yourself time to adjust, and you will surely get the hang of it. Thanks to the natural gift of adaptability, you will learn to adapt soon naturally.

This game requires you to stay calm, stay strong, and be in control of your life. No matter what circumstances may be, know that there is a solution for you. It may not be easy as the easy way usually results in bad results. However, the good news is that creating an alter ego is not difficult as long as you do it properly. You have a choice: you can face life and your work only as who you are risking your true self or you can create an alter ego and make life easier to deal with and be happier for you. Your choice.

Creating and Programming Your Alter Ego

Now comes a very interesting part as we are now going to talk about the actual steps of creating an alter ego. Creating an alter ego is easy and fun. It is just like playing a game. If you are familiar with roleplaying games, then it is very much the same, except that this alter ego will be playing in the "real" world instead of a computer or tabletop game.

To create your alter ego, it is a good practice to write it down. So, get a pen and paper and prepare to write your alter ego. The first step is to program it. Programming is the process of defining your alter ego, such as who it is going to be, the things that it will do, its functions, how you want it to behave and think, among others.

First, write down the name of your alter ego. You can give it any name that you want. You can also use the same name as your name but adding 2 at the end. For example, *(your name) 2.* This way, you know that when you say that name, it is your alter ego that is being referred to and not your true self.

Next, write down the work that your alter ego will be engaged in. After that, write down what your alter ego is going to be like, such as its attitude, behavior, and so on. Take note that this is all referring to your alter ego and not your true self. You may make your alter ego to have the same characteristics as your true self, but I would say that its personality may have to adjust to the work that it has to do, as well as the kind of situation and people that it has to deal with.

Although not necessary, you may also give a history to your alter ego, more its past story or where it is coming from. Its story may extremely vary from your real life story. Feel free to be creative to make your alter ego as real as it can be. Again, this is just like playing a roleplaying tabletop game. You do not have to be too serious. Have as much fun as you like.

Although not necessary, you may also add the image of your alter ego. This is how you are going to look when you are using your alter ego. Of course, this will all be in your imagination, which means that you have complete freedom how you want your alter ego to look. This is also a good practice but not required. Do you want to imagine yourself wearing glasses or perhaps you want to look like a completely different person? If you want, you may look like a dragon. Do not be shy to express your creativity with your imagination. You can also always change into another appearance later on at any time. As for me, I do not really use a different image. I focus more on the very essence. After all, the image is just a shell. But, feel free to make good use of this technique if you want.

Last but not least, you can write more details about your alter ego if you want. The more that you know who your alter ego is, the more effective it will be, and the easier it will be to shift between your true self and your alter ego. Do not rush this process. Feel free to spend as much time as you may need. You also do not have to worry since you can make adjustments and changes to your alter ego later on if ever necessary. You are totally in control.

Once you are done, be sure to keep your notes private as you would not want other people to know your alter ego very well. In fact, once the personality of your alter ego has been established, you can burn your notes to keep the identity of your alter ego safe from prying eyes.

Now that you have programmed your alter ego, it is now time to activate it.

Activating Your Alter Ego

The next step is to activate your alter ego. This is the part where you finally and actually assume your alter ego. You will now be using it in the "real" world. This is the shift from your true self into the self of your alter ego.

There are various ways to shift into your alter ego. In fact, there are no hard and fast rules on how to go about doing this. The key here is to be able to shift your mind from your true self and into the mind or consciousness of your alter ego. You will put your true self to sleep as you shift into your alter ego. It is important to master this because you will be doing this countless times. Do not worry as this is easy to do. It may be quite challenging in the beginning; but with continuous practice, you will surely get the hang of it.

A simple way to activate your alter ego and make the switch is by saying the name of your alter ego. You can also add the word *activated* at the end. For example, *(name of your alter ego) activated*. You do not really have to say it out loud. You can just say it silently in your mind. This effort can help to communicate to your mind that you are now going to make the shift from your true self into your alter ego.

Another approach is to imagine yourself now assuming the image of your alter ego (in case you have created a separate appearance for your alter ego). You can also simply make your awareness shift from your true self and into your alter ego.

A snap of your fingers can also be used to signal the shift from your true self into your alter ego. Any signal can be used. The important thing is to know with your mind that you are now making the shift and that you are now assuming the self of your alter ego. When this happens, you should totally forget about your true self. Put it to sleep as you assume your alter ego. You only have one body, and this body can only accommodate one self at a time. When you shift into your alter ego, the true self must be put to sleep, and vice versa. Your two selves have to take turns whenever needed.

There are really no strict rules on how to do this. The important thing is to know in your mind that you are now making the shift and that you are now assuming the identity of your alter ego.

In the beginning, this conscious shift from your true self and into your alter ego can help greatly. However, once you get used to using your alter ego, you can shift into it smoothly and naturally even without any signal any more that you are going to assume your alter ego. It will all just be a matter of will and intention. Still, if you are just starting out, it is good to use a signal to communicate the shift.

Playing the Role of Your Alter Ego

Now that you have made the shift into your alter ego, you can now play using this character. Do not forget that once you make the shift, you should let go of your other self completely. This is just like playing a tabletop game where you forget about the world and just focus on the game as you move along with it using your in-game character. Now that you have assumed your alter ego, your true self is now asleep, and you are now completely absorbed into the character and identity of your alter ego.

Just playing along with the role of your alter ego. Let your alter ego come to life. Think and act as your alter ego. We have already defined who your alter ego is by now, so it is just a matter of roleplaying as your alter ego.

Now, know that whatever your alter ego does and whatever stress and pressures it is facing, it is facing it on its own. Your true self is not connected to your alter ego. In fact, it is now asleep while you are playing the role of your alter ego. So, do not worry about what happens while you are in your alter ego. Still, this does not mean that you can just do whatever you want and be irresponsible. Your alter ego has a certain personality that would fit the job right and to handle the work problems effectively. Just continue with the game as your alter ego and enjoy it as much as you.

You are just playing along. Your true self can be asleep or it can simply watch how your alter ego is doing just like when you are playing a game where you are aware of your real self and that you are only watching over your in-game character as you enjoy the game and all the challenges along the way.

By doing this, you become detached from the work, as well as from all the stress and worries that usually come along with it.

Putting your true self to sleep should not be taken literally. It only means that when you are in your alter ego, your true self must not interfere with it nor should it care so much about it. Instead, your true self should only be a passive observer. This is just like playing a tabletop game where you only observe and enjoy your in-game character. Even if your in-game character is having a hard time, it does not mean that you should be personally affected. Instead, just enjoy the game.

You must understand that it is already an unavoidable certainty that your alter ego will face so much stress and problems. In fact, this is one of the main reasons why you have created your alter ego in the first place. However, you must realize that challenges are a part of life, and they can be fun. In fact, tabletop games are interesting because you have to go through an adventure, which adventure necessarily entails taking on problems and challenges along the way. The same principle applies with your alter ego. However, in this case, your true self remains pure and undefiled regardless of what happens to your alter ego.

It should be clarified that when you are in your alter ego, it does not mean that you should not care. You must still do your work properly with diligence. You do not need to aim for perfection as that can also be stressful, but at least do your work properly. After all, it is expected that you have programmed your alter ego to work effectively.

When you are playing the role of your alter ego, just enjoy every moment of it. The stress and problems are all part of the game. So, just enjoy the game of life and let your alter ego handle all the stress and worries.

Shifting Back to Your True Self

When you are done with the day's or night's work, you can safely and easily shift back to your true self. Shifting back to your true self is very easy, and it is just like shifting to your alter ego. For this purpose, you can also use signal words, such as by saying, *Alter ego deactivated* or *(Your real name signifying your true self)*. Feel free to come up with your own statement to signify the return to your true self. In fact, in many instances, you would not even have to do this. The important thing is to know in your mind that you are going to take a break from the game and that you are now going back to your true self. This is just a matter of will and intention.

You should get used to shifting back and forth from your true self into your alter ego, and vice versa, as you will be doing this countless times. Do not worry, this is very easy to do. With just some practice, you will surely get the hang of it after some time.

Whether you function as your true self or as your alter ego is just a simple shift in the mind. The important thing to remember is not to confuse the two selves that you have and to not allow one self to interfere with the other. This is not difficult to do; and with enough practice, everything will be as smooth as a flowing river.

Make Adjustments to Your Alter Ego

As you play the game, know that you can always make adjustments to your alter ego. Depending on the situation at work and the matters that you have to deal with, you may have to reprogram your alter ego. You may revise your written notes (the one that you made when you created your alter ego), or you can simply do the adjustments as you move along even without a written record of it. The important thing here is not to forget what your alter ego is like. This way, you will not confuse your two selves.

There are no rules on how you should make the adjustments as this will depend on your needs and how you want to play your role in the game. The important thing here is to know that you can always make adjustments or changes to your alter ego to make it more effective, as well as to make the adventure more enjoyable for you.

Time Management

Let us now discuss another important subject: time management. We have to understand that in this game of life, there is the element of time that we have to consider. You must have enough time for your true self and enough time for your alter ego. There are no strict rules on how to go about this because it will depend on your personal circumstances and current situation. But, this is not difficult to define. This is as simple as knowing that time for work will be exclusively for your alter ego and all time outside of work will be especially for your true self. Just be sure to manage your work schedule so that you will have more time for your true self.

When it comes to time management, it really helps to be organized. When it comes to being organized, it helps to write things down when possible. This way, you can always think outside the box.

You should also avoid multitasking. Many people these days find the idea of multitasking quite cool, but it can be damaging to your mental health in the long run. It is okay to multitask if you are doing something fun that you enjoy; but if you are multitasking between one problem and another, this will be a problem—and it can be very stressful.

A slow living approach to life can also help significantly. Be present in the moment of now and live your life with more intention and awareness. Do not take any moment for granted, especially when you are in your true self.

As much as possible, make more time for your true self, but also be sure to give enough time for you to do all the work that needs to be done. Avoid procrastinating. Procrastination is a terrible habit, and you must never fall into that trap.

Once you have enough time for your work as your alter ego and enough time for your true self, things will flow much more smoothly and peacefully for you.

Non-Attachment

The idea of non-attachment is a popular teaching in Buddhism, but it is also present in Christianity, as well as in other religions. In fact, you do not even need to be associated with any religion to practice non-attachment. Non-attachment is a spiritual teaching, so it covers all walks of life.

Non-attachment does not mean that you should not care. It also comes with the realization of death and that all things are impermanent. All your problems and worries at work will not last. Many years from now, it is as if they did not even exist. So, instead of focusing too much on them and allowing yourself to be stressed out and unhappy, let your alter ego deal with them as your true self spends quality time with your family and loved ones.

You should also practice non-attachment to your alter ego. Your alter ego is only your in-game character in the game of this world. This way, your true self will not be affected with the worries and stress that your alter ego will go through during the game. Life is a grand adventure, and this is how we play it with an alter ego.

This book teaches non-attachment not on a purely spiritual level but more about your alter ego. You should not be attached to your alter ego. This way, your true self will not have to experience the hardships that your alter ego will be going through. Especially if the nature of your work involves dealing with people, stress levels can get high. You must protect your true self from all these, and which is precisely why you have an alter ego.

So how do you exercise non-attachment to your alter ego? It is as simple as seeing your alter ego as a completely separate self from your true self. Again, a good piece of advice is to view your work as a game, and your alter ego is simply your in-game character. Just like any game, there will be challenges. You will be fighting dragons. Let your alter ego handle all these things as you let your true self be who you really are and enjoy life to the fullest.

You do not have to worry so much about your alter ego. It can function without you having to fear anything. It cannot die as it is a creation of the mind. As your alter ego goes through the adventure, let it have a good time as well, enjoying every challenge and problem along the way. After all, if there are no challenges and hardships, then it means that you are not playing a game.

Another application of non-attachment is with the work itself. Although people these days want to be in control, and even delude themselves into thinking that they are in control, the truth is that we are really not in control of anything. The control that we think we have is a mere illusion. There are many variables in life. No matter how modern the world seems to have become, we are still in the jungle—because this is the truth of nature.

The only thing that can be said to be under our control is the very work that we do; but how people would respond and think, among others, these things are way out of our control. If we depend our happiness on what other people think, then we are giving them the power to decide whether we will be happy or not. Unfortunately, the fact is that the world is full of vile and selfish people, and it would not be a wise decision to depend your happiness on other people. Do not feel so bad as this actually makes the game much more interesting. Even in tabletop games, we use the dice to direct the fate of our character. The same can be said about the "real" life game. So, practice non-attachment, and you will surely save yourself from much unnecessary fear, worries, and stress. Enjoy the adventure with your alter ego.

Should You Tell People About Your Alter Ego?

It depends on you. Personally, I think that it is better not to tell people about it as they may not understand it and only think of you in a strange way. So many people these days are also very judgmental—and they are judgmental in a negative way. To avoid unnecessary complications, it is recommended that you just keep it to yourself.

You can share about it with those who are very close to you and only with those whom you can completely trust. Of course, when you do this, you would have to be your true self. It is quite awkward for your alter ego to be the one admitting that it is just an alter ego. Moreover, when you take the place of your alter ego, you should not be concerned about this matter as your focus should be on the game (work)—so just stay in the game and play it the best way you can and with as much fun as you can get from it.

Many people will also not understand this concept, so it is best to just keep quiet and just keep it to yourself. They might also be offended at work if you tell them that you are just there as your alter ego, and that they do not really know who you really are. Hence, to avoid unnecessary problems and complications, it is best not to tell people about it, especially those that belong to the game (work).

"Real" Life Game

What is real? What is real to you may not be real to another. Your work as a game only has a reality that you give to it. If what is real to you is only limited by what you can see or touch, then that would be a shallow way of looking at things. In fact, if we think about it, the wonderful things in life could not even be seen or touched by the physical senses, such as happiness, peace, forgiveness, kindness, holiness, and love, among others.

In this world, we often hear people saying "real world", and it is as if it is the only thing that matters. But, what is the "real" world to you? What is real for someone may not be real for another. Or, what may be important to someone may not be as important to another. In the end, what the "real world" means and just how important it is would depend on you. It will depend on how much significance and value that you give to it.

When we use an alter ego, we have a choice. We can make our work appear lighter by considering it as a game while we are in our alter ego, and that the only real life that truly truly matters is the one where we are our real self. How much importance you want to give to the world that involves your alter ego would depend on you. As for me, I prefer to not take the game seriously at all. Of course, this does not mean that I would not do my job properly. There is a big difference between not taking it seriously and being extremely irresponsible.

There is nothing wrong with not taking your work seriously. In fact, it is even a common advice not to take life seriously. After all, we are not going out of it alive. So, instead of stressing out, just enjoy the adventure as much as we could.

In another view, both lives are actually real. Your life as your real self and your life as your alter ego are real. Still, a big difference is where you put your focus on and which one you consider to be important to you. As for me, although I do my work responsibly and well, I give more focus and importance to the life of my real self. One's preference will most likely vary depending on your personal circumstances. So, spend as much time as you may need to weigh the situation and use that knowledge to help you balance your life as your alter ego and as your real self.

According to the great writer, William Shakespeare, all the world is a stage and that we are merely players or actors on that stage. When we create an alter ego, we intentionally create our actor that we will be using to fill in the role for that stage play.

Can You Create More Than One Alter Ego?

The answer to this question is a resounding yes. However, this is something that you might want to avoid as much as possible. The reason for this is that we must not forget that as we operate in this world, regardless of the self that we assume, there is still the element of time. If you create so many alter egos, you may not have enough time to satisfy all your selves.

If you are lucky and if you are living an ideal life, then perhaps you may not even need to create an alter ego, which is a very good thing. However, the truth is that many people these days would want to have an alter ego to protect their true self, as well as to maintain peace of mind. A good piece of advice is to try to face your life first without an alter ego. If you find that there is something wrong with it, then try to create an alter ego and see how it works for you.

Personally, I strongly suggest that you limit it to just having one alter ego. In this regard, you must manage your time effectively. There are times when you may have to sacrifice some things so that you can have enough time for your true self.

Keep in mind that the things that you do in life will always take some of your precious time. If you are busy with so many things, you will need so much time in your hands, which you might not have. For example, I used to have many hobbies. I easily like many things. However, I noticed that I was already doing so many different things in a day that I did not have enough time to really focus and live my true self. As a solution, I limited the things that I would keep in my life and let go of the things that I do not need and those that I can live without. This is just a personal example, but the principle remains the same. We need to manage our time well if we want to keep our true self happy and satisfied; and sometimes, this may mean making sacrifices for our own good, as well as for the good of our loved ones.

How to Be Happy As Your Alter Ego

The moments that you spend as your alter ego should not be a torture. It is already a blessing that you have work. Many people are looking for work but fail to get hired. So, it is already a good thing that you are currently working.

It is good if you are engaged in the line of work that you really want—something that you are personally passionate about. In fact, if your work is also something that you are personally passionate about, then you might no longer need an alter ego. But, the sad truth is that many people are also engaged in a work that they do not want. They are just there only for the money. Still, it is good to know that every kind of legitimate work is a form of service to others. By engaging in your work, you can help people and make this world a beautiful place.

It is a good piece of advice to see the beauty of your work. Think about the people that you are able to help because of your work.

It should also be clarified that time spent as your alter ego does not mean that you should be miserable. Again, it is a game that you are playing. You should enjoy it.

Let your alter ego enjoy the game that it is playing. It does not matter how you do this, but the point here is to appreciate the joy of your work as it is. Sometimes all that we need is to view our work from a different angle to see that it is a blessing.

On Spirituality

If you are not a spiritual person, then you may skip this part. If you are a spiritual person, regardless of your religion or even if you do not associate yourself with any religion, then know that it really helps to deal with life in a spiritual way. A saint once said that we cannot truly be happy by pursuing after material things. This is because we are made in the image and likeness of God. As such, the only way to truly be happy and satisfied is by giving the soul what it needs—and that is to be united with God.

In this regard, I strongly recommend that you look into the teachings of Jesus Christ. There was a time in my life when I was severely depressed and suicidal, and it was Jesus who saved me.

Living this life with Christ also makes it so much lighter. In fact, if you have enough faith, you would not even have to worry about anything at all. I am not a saint, but I can honestly say that all of your work problems and all of your problems literally are nothing as compared with the love of Jesus Christ.

Living as a soul will also help you have a better and deeper view of this life. It is also a good way not to be affected by the problems that this world offers. But, this is a choice that you have to make. As for me, I can say that it has significantly helped me and that is why I am sharing this here.

You do not need to be a member of any religion to follow Christ. I suggest that you seek Him in your own way. It is highly recommended to read the Bible on your own, especially the Book of Matthew, which also happens to be the first book in the New Testament of the Bible. This is an excellent way to learn the life and divine teachings of the Master (Jesus Christ). Once you start following Christ, you can rest assured that you will never be alone in this life again. He will always be with you, and He will help you with all your problems. Just give it a try and see how it works for you.

A Message

By now, you should already be equipped with all the knowledge that you need to create an alter ego. Having an alter ego can significantly help you have peace of mind, which leads to happiness. Indeed, the world, especially as it is now, can be a difficult place to live in. Know that you are not alone. There are many people who are having a hard time in this world. You must not give up. You should stay strong and remain good. Do not let the world change who you really are. If things get too difficult, let your alter ego deal with those things, and be sure to protect your true self from the world.

It may take some time before you get used to having an alter ego. It usually takes a few days to a few weeks before you can get used to it. Just stay strong and do not give up. Keep practicing, and you will surely get the hang of it soon—and you will be thankful that you have chosen not to give up.

No matter what your situation in life is right now, know that you deserve to be happy. Now is the time to be free from the evils of the world. Be happy, be you, and be free.

About the Author

Www.charlzdelacruz.com
Password to enter the private page: ANGEL912

CHARLES MAGE

Don't miss out!

Visit the website below and you can sign up to receive emails whenever Charles Mage publishes a new book. There's no charge and no obligation.

https://books2read.com/r/B-A-SXMH-CFKAC

BOOKS 2 READ

Connecting independent readers to independent writers.

Did you love *Create an Alter Ego for Work Success and Peace of Mind*? Then you should read *My Magickal Rosary Journey*[1] by Charles Mage!

My Magickal Rosary Journey is my personal journey of magic through the Rosary. It is a journey from doubt to faith, from the mundane to the magical, and from meaningless power into love and everything that has a soul.

This journey is not just my journey, but it is also for everyone who seeks for true spirituality. Whether you are someone who seeks to experience God or a magical practitioner who wants

---

1. https://books2read.com/u/b6OE8p

2. https://books2read.com/u/b6OE8p

to deepen your current spiritual level, then this humble journey might be able to share with you some light that leads to the truth.

My Magickal Rosary Journey is a journey of a soul, and it is a journey that all souls can take. All that we need to do is to have a leap of faith and allow the magic of the universe to manifest in our lives.

How is the Rosary related to the occult arts of magick? This is something that many people wonder about. The truth is that the Rosary is naturally magical in and of itself. Moreover, when a person prays, regardless of the prayer that is used, as long as it is a prayer of the heart, then it has the power to reach, touch, and even move, the heart of God.

A monk once said that all true prayers are considered high magic for they are prayers that elevate one's soul and connect them to the Divine Source. Indeed, there is so much power and magic in the Rosary, if you know how to pray it properly and if you actually do so regularly.

My Magickal Rosary Journey also shares about the inner truth of humanity as one struggles in spiritual life and through this world. We will talk about the magic of the Rosary, the shifting of the mind from pure desire for power into what is magical and meaningful.

This is our journey --- and it is a journey that can change one's life forever. May you find in this handbook the light that leads to truth, magick, and love.

Read more at https://www.charlzdelacruz.com/.

Also by Charles Mage

Magickal Imagination: Learn to Use Your Imagination in a Magickal and Witchy Way

Dowsing the Casino: Make Money Dowsing

Magickal Partnership

Energy Ball Manual

Sex Magick for the Solitary Practitioner

Elemental Invocation

Vampirism Magick for Beginners

Vril Mastery: Harness the Force of the Gods

Psi Constructs

The Magickal Mindset

Instant Magick for Everyday Use

Healing with Psi

Magick as a Way of Life

Dowsing Without Tools

Learn to Create an Astral Temple

Fun Things to Do with Your Energy Ball

In Search of Beauty

Imagination Magick: Learn to Use Your Imagination to Live a Magickal Life

Pendulum Magick: Communicate with Spirits

Magick in Your Pocket: Magical Spells You Can Cast Anywhere, Even in Your Pocket!

Make Your Own Magick Wand The Intuitive Way
The Way of the Magus
The Secret Occult Techniques of Making and Using a Ouija
Board
Mistakes and Pitfalls in Magical Practice
The Magick of the Zenina Circle
Escape Life with Your Imagination
Experiments with Magical Energy
Elemental Magick of the Five Fingers
Magical Keys to Self-Empowerment
How to Acquire & Take Care of Magickal Creatures
Beat the Casino Using Clairvoyance
The Magical Art of Mental Projection
Mindcraft Spells Starter Manual
The Magick of the Holy Rosary
How the Rosary Changed My Life and How It Can Change
Yours Too
True Initiation into the Craft of Magick
The Way of the Pendulum
The Christian Magician
Shamanic Journey for Beginners
Life Lessons from a Butterfly
Psychokinesis Manual to Beat the Casino and Make Money
Phone Sex Magick
The Magick of Writing
Energy Servitor Manual
My Magickal Rosary Journey
How to Create an Elemental Servitor
Basic Wizardry 101
Create an Alter Ego for Work Success and Peace of Mind